KID'S SETS
OPTIONS

LEISURE ARTS, INC.
Little Rock, Arkansas

EDITORIAL STAFF

Vice President and Editor-in-Chief: Sandra Graham Case. *Executive Director of Publications:* Cheryl Nodine Gunnells. *Senior Director of Publications:* Susan White Sullivan. *Director of Designer Relations:* Debra Nettles. *Director of Retail Marketing:* Stephen Wilson. *Art Operations Director:* Jeff Curtis. *Special Projects Coordinator:* Mary Sullivan Hutcheson. TECHNICAL — *Technical Writer:* Lois J. Long. *Editorial Writer:* Susan McManus Johnson. ART — *Art Publications Director:* Rhonda Hodge Shelby. *Art Imaging Director:* Mark Hawkins. *Senior Publications Designer:* Dana Vaughn. *Imaging Technician:* Mark R. Potter. *Photography Stylist:* Cassie Francioni. *Contributing Photographer:* Jason Masters. *Publishing Systems Administrator:* Becky Riddle. *Publishing Systems Assistants:* Clint Hanson, Josh Hyatt, and John Rose.

BUSINESS STAFF

Chief Operating Officer: Tom Siebenmorgen. *Vice President, Sales and Marketing:* Pam Stebbins. *Director of Sales and Services:* Margaret Reinold. *Vice President, Operations:* Jim Dittrich. *Comptroller, Operations:* Rob Thieme. *Retail Customer Service Manager:* Stan Raynor. *Print Production Manager:* Fred F. Pruss.

Made in the United States of America.

ISBN 1-57486-588-9

10 9 8 7 6 5 4 3 2 1

OPTIONS

You've just found the **perfect** patterns for your little girl's knit fashions.

Wouldn't you like to be sure the yarn is just as perfect? To help you see the results you would get from a second yarn choice, this exciting **Options** book shows you two versions of the same outfit in entirely different brands and colors of yarn.

Two of these three winter ensembles by designer Laura Polley includes girls' sizes two through six, with the last set in sizes four through ten. Choose a jacket, a poncho, or a coat; then create a matching hat, scarf, and a muff or mittens.

Now you'll create knitwear that's (almost) as special as she is!

meet
LauraPolley

"I've been designing in one form or another since the age of five,"

says Laura Polley. "That was when my drawing of a bonnet-clad turtle appeared in an issue of *Highlights* magazine."

Laura says her childhood was spent drawing, writing poetry, and searching for self-expression. "But I still yearned for my own creative niche."

Laura found that niche at the age of eighteen. As an exchange student in central Mexico, she watched as women all around her created vibrant, colorful sweaters with wool yarn and needles. Laura felt drawn to the craft, and that it

"spoke to her." That was when Laura realized she had to learn the skill. So she plunged into the world of knitting, teaching herself from a needlework book. She collected every pattern magazine she could find and tested her skills at every opportunity, until one day she began creating her own knit designs.

Laura now has her own design company, Good Fiberations!, and many of her published designs can be seen on her Website, www.goodfiberations.com.

"I'm still passionate about yarn and knitting," Laura admits, "and I still collect knitting-related books. I find inspiration in almost everything, from house paint to grand landscapes of nature. I believe that every yarn has a voice, and will announce its purpose to you, if you only pay attention. The yarn knows what it wants to be!

"For me, designing is a necessary part of life..."

"For me, designing is a necessary part of life, filling every day with color, texture, and inspiration. More importantly, designing fulfills my lifelong desire to connect and communicate with others. How wonderful to speak with yarn and needles!"

DENIM QUARTET   PAGE 8

DE COLORES   PAGE 20

NEVER A PATCH ON YOU   PAGE 28

GENERAL
INSTRUCTIONS
PAGE 40

DENIM QUARTET

OPTION

1

Pink is especially sweet on this cozy **quartet** of outerwear items knit with eyelash and bulky weight yarns. A denim-inspired jacket, soft muff, narrow scarf, and **"furry"** hat will keep her warm in style.

OPTION ②

Blue is the traditional color for **denim**, but real denim has never looked this **nice**! Knit the four-piece ensemble using a slightly shorter eyelash yarn to make it truly **plush**.

Option 1

Plymouth Yarn Galway MEDIUM 4
Medium/Worsted Weight Yarn
[3½ ounces, 210 yards (100 grams, 192 meters) per skein]
  MC: #135 Lt Pink - 4{4-5-6} skeins
  Color A: #125 Dk Pink - 1 skein

Adriafil® Stars
Medium/Worsted Weight Short Eyelash Yarn
[1¾ ounces, 69 yards (50 grams, 63 meters) per skein]
  Color B: #83 Lt Pink - 3{3-3-4} skeins

Plymouth Yarn Colorlash
Carrying Weight Eyelash Yarn
[1¾ ounces, 220 yards (50 grams, 201 meters) per skein]
  Color B: #37 Dk Pink - 1{1-1-2} skein(s)

Note: "Color B" is one strand each of medium/worsted weight short eyelash yarn and carrying weight eyelash yarn held together throughout.

Straight knitting needles, sizes 6 (4 mm), 8 (5 mm),
  and 9 (5.5 mm) **or** sizes needed for gauge
¾" (19 mm) Buttons - 4{5-5-6}
Sewing needle and thread
Yarn needle

DENIM QUARTET ■■■▭ INTERMEDIATE

Option 2

Lion Brand® Wool-Ease® MEDIUM 4
Medium/Worsted Weight Yarn
[3 ounces, 197 yards (85 grams, 180 meters) per skein]
  MC: #114 Denim - 4{5-5-6} skeins
  Color A: #171 Gold - 1 skein

Lion Brand® Fun Fur BULKY 5
Bulky Weight Eyelash Yarn
[1½ ounces, 57 yards (40 grams, 52 meters) per skein]
  Color B: #203 Indigo - 3{4-4-4} skeins

Straight knitting needles, sizes 6 (4 mm), 8 (5 mm),
  and 9 (5.5 mm) **or** sizes needed for gauge
¾" (19 mm) Buttons - 4{5-5-6}
Sewing needle and thread
Yarn needle

SIZES: 2{4-6-8}

Note: Instructions are written for size 2 with sizes 4, 6, and 8 in braces { }. Instructions will be easier to read if you circle all the numbers pertaining to your child's size. If only one number is given, it applies to all sizes.

FINISHED MEASUREMENTS

JACKET
Finished Chest Measurement:
26{27$^1/_2$-29$^1/_2$-31}"/66{70-75-78.5} cm

HAT
Finished Circumference:
17{17-18$^3/_4$-18$^3/_4$}"/43{43-47.5-47.5} cm

MUFF
Finished Measurements:
7$^1/_2${8-8$^1/_2$-9}" around x 8{9$^1/_2$-10-11}" long/
19{20.5-21.5-23} cm x 20.5{24-25.5-28} cm

SCARF
Finished Measurements:
4{5-5-6}" wide x 37$^1/_2${41$^1/_2$-45-49}" long/
10{12.5-12.5-15} cm x 95.5{105.5-114.5-124.5} cm

GAUGES

With medium size needles and MC,
in Stockinette Stitch,
18 sts and 24 rows = 4" (10 cm)
with largest size needles and Color B,
in Garter Stitch (knit every row),
16 sts and 36 rows = 4" (10 cm)

Instructions begin on page 12.

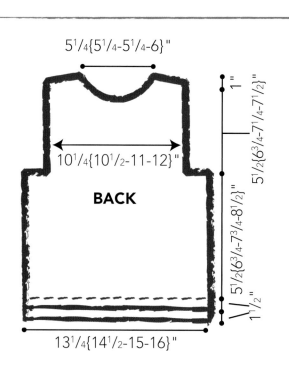

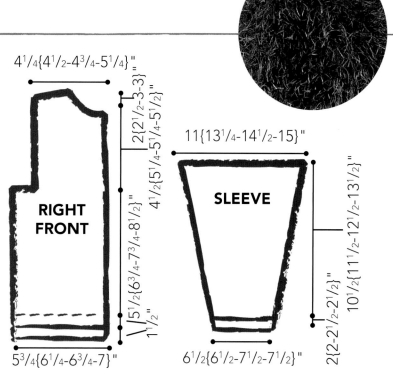

JACKET
BACK
HEM
With smallest size needles and MC, cast on 60{64-68-72} sts.

Work in Stockinette Stitch for 1¹⁄₂" (4 cm), ending by working a **wrong** side row.

Turning Ridge: Purl across.

BODY
Change to medium size needles.

Work even until Back measures 3" (7.5 cm) from cast on edge, ending by working a **wrong** side row.

Ridge Row: K2, (slip 1 as if to **purl** with yarn in front, K1) across.

Work even until Back measures approximately 5¹⁄₂{6³⁄₄-7³⁄₄-8¹⁄₂}"/14{17-19.5-21.5} cm from Ridge Row, ending by working a **wrong** side row.

Armhole Shaping
Rows 1 and 2: Bind off 7{8-9-9} sts, work across: 46{48-50-54} sts.

Work even until Armholes measure approximately 5¹⁄₂{6³⁄₄-7¹⁄₄-7¹⁄₂}"/14{17-18.5-19} cm, ending by working a **wrong** side row.

Neck Shaping
Both sides of Neck are worked at same time using separate yarn for **each** side.

Row 1: K 14{15-16-16}; with second yarn, bind off next 18{18-18-22} sts, knit across: 14{15-16-16} sts **each** side.

Row 2: Purl across to within 3 sts of Neck edge, SSP (*Fig. 10, page 46*), P1; with second yarn, P1, P2 tog (*Fig. 9, page 45*), purl across: 13{14-15-15} sts **each** side.

Shoulder Shaping
Row 1: Bind off 5 sts, knit across to within 3 sts of Neck edge, K2 tog (*Fig. 7, page 44*), K1; with second yarn, K1, SSK (*Figs. 8a-c, page 45*), knit across.

Row 2: Bind off 5 sts, purl across; with second yarn, purl across: 7{8-9-9} sts **each** side.

Row 3: Bind off 3{4-5-5} sts, K2 tog, K1; with second yarn, K1, SSK, knit across.

Row 4: Bind off 3{4-5-5} sts, purl across; with second yarn, purl across: 3 sts **each** side.

Row 5: Bind off 3 sts; with second yarn, knit across.

Bind of remaining sts.

RIGHT FRONT
With smallest size needles and MC, cast on 26{28-30-32} sts.

Work same as Back until Right Front measures same as Back to Armhole Shaping, ending by working a **right** side row.

Armhole Shaping
Row 1: Bind off 7{8-9-9} sts, purl across: 19{20-21-23} sts.

Work even until Armhole measures approximately 4¹⁄₂{5¹⁄₄-5¹⁄₄-5¹⁄₂}"/11.5{13.5-13.5-14} cm, ending by working a **wrong** side row.

Neck Shaping
Row 1: Bind off 6{6-6-8} sts, knit across: 13{14-15-15} sts.

Row 2: Purl across.

Row 3 (Decrease row)**:** K1, SSK, knit across: 12{13-14-14} sts.

Rows 4 and 5: Repeat Rows 2 and 3: 11{12-13-13} sts.

Work even until Right Front measures same as Back to Shoulder Shaping, ending by working a **right** side row.

Shoulder Shaping
Row 1: Bind off 5 sts, purl across: 6{7-8-8} sts.

Row 2: Knit across.

Row 3: Bind off 3{4-5-5} sts, purl across: 3 sts.

Row 4: Knit across.

Bind off remaining sts.

LEFT FRONT
With smallest size needles and MC, cast on 26{28-30-32} sts.

Work same as Back until Left Front measures same as Back to Armhole Shaping, ending by working a **wrong** side row.

Armhole Shaping
Row 1: Bind off 7{8-9-9} sts, knit across: 19{20-21-23} sts.

Work even until Armhole measures same as Right Front to Neck Shaping, ending by working a **right** side row.

Neck Shaping
Row 1: Bind off 6{6-6-8} sts, purl across: 13{14-15-15} sts.

Row 2: Knit across.

Row 3 (Decrease row)**:** P1, P2 tog, purl across: 12{13-14-14} sts.

Rows 4 and 5: Repeat Rows 2 and 3: 11{12-13-13} sts.

Work even until Left Front measures same as Right Front to Shoulder Shaping, ending by working a **wrong** side row.

Shoulder Shaping
Row 1: Bind off 5 sts, knit across: 6{7-8-8} sts.

Row 2: Purl across.

Row 3: Bind off 3{4-5-5} sts, knit across: 3 sts.

Row 4: Purl across.

Bind off remaining sts.

Instructions continued on page 14.

SLEEVE (Make 2)
CUFF
With largest size needles and Color B, cast on 26{26-30-30} sts.

Work in Garter Stitch (knit every row) for 2{2-2$\frac{1}{2}$-2$\frac{1}{2}$}"/5{5-6.5-6.5} cm, ending by working a **wrong** side row; cut Color B.

BODY
Change to medium size needles and MC.

Row 1: Knit across increasing 4 sts evenly spaced *(see Increasing Evenly and Figs. 2a & b, page 42)*: 30{30-34-34} sts.

Row 2: Purl across.

Row 3 - Ridge Row: K2, (slip 1 as if to **purl** with yarn in front, K1) across.

Work in Stockinette Stitch, increasing one stitch at **each** edge, every other row, 4{9-10-11} times; then increase every fourth row, 6 times: 50{60-66-68} sts.

Work even until Sleeve measures approximately 12$\frac{1}{2}${13$\frac{1}{2}$-15-16}"/32{34.5-38-40.5} cm from cast on edge, ending by working a **wrong** side row.

Bind off all sts.

POCKET (Make 4)
With medium size needles and MC, cast on 11{11-13-15} sts.

Row 1: Knit across.

Row 2: Purl across.

Row 3 - Ridge Row: K1, (slip 1 as if to **purl** with yarn in front, K1) across.

Short Row Shaping
To "wrap" a stitch, drop yarn, slip next stitch as if to **purl**, bring yarn to opposite side of work from where it was left, replace slipped stitch on left needle, bring yarn back to opposite side of work, thus wrapping the stitch.

Row 1: Purl across to last 3 sts, wrap next st, **turn**.

Row 2: Knit across to last 3 sts, wrap next st, **turn**.

Row 3: Purl across to last 3 sts, insert right needle under the wrap from back to front. Lift wrap onto left needle without removing right needle from it, then purl wrap and st tog, P2.

Row 4: Knit across to last 3 sts, insert right needle under the wrap, then into the st as usual, and knit wrap and st tog, K2.

Work even until Pocket measures 3" (7.5 cm) from cast on edge, ending by working a **wrong** side row.

Ridge Row: K1, (slip 1 as if to **purl** with yarn in front, K1) across.

Work even until Pocket measures 4" (10 cm) from cast on edge, ending by working a **wrong** side row.

Change to smallest size needles.

Turning Ridge: Purl across.

Work in Stockinette Stitch for 1" (2.5 cm).

Bind off all sts.

Using photo as a guide, thread yarn needle with Color A and weave needle through sts over slipped sts on Ridge Rows.

Fold top edge of Pocket to **wrong** side along Turning Ridge and whipstitch in place (*Fig. 12, page 46*).

BUTTON BAND
Fold lower edge of Left Front to **wrong** side along Turning Ridge for hem and pin in place at front opening.

With **right** side facing, medium size needles and MC, pick up 48{54-58-62} sts evenly spaced along Left Front edge (*Fig. 11a, page 46*), picking up through both thicknesses of hem.

Row 1: Purl across.

Row 2 - Ridge Row: (K1, slip 1 as if to **purl** with yarn in front) across to last 2 sts, K2.

Work 7 rows in Stockinette Stitch, ending by working a **wrong** side row.

Change to smallest size needles.

Turning Ridge: Purl across.

Work 9 rows in Stockinette Stitch.

Bind off all sts in **knit**.

Thread yarn needle with Color A and weave needle through sts over slipped sts on Ridge Row.

Fold Button Band to **wrong** side along Turning Ridge and whipstitch in place.

BUTTONHOLE BAND
Fold lower edge of Right Front to **wrong** side along Turning Ridge for hem and pin in place at front opening.

With **right** side facing, medium size needles and MC, pick up 48{54-58-62} sts evenly spaced along Right Front edge, picking up through both thicknesses of hem.

Row 1: Purl across.

Row 2 - Ridge Row: K2, (slip 1 as if to **purl** with yarn in front, K1) across.

Row 3: Purl across.

Mark placement of buttonholes, placing markers 1/2" (12 mm) from neck edge and 1" (2.5 cm) from bottom edge. Evenly space 2{3-3-4} markers for remaining buttons.

Row 4 (Buttonhole row): ★ Knit across to next marker, remove marker, bind off next 2 sts; repeat from ★ 3{4-4-5} times **more**, knit across.

Row 5 (Buttonhole row): ★ Purl across to bound off sts, **turn**; add on 2 sts (*Figs. 5a & b, page 43*), **turn**; repeat from ★ 3{4-4-5} times **more**, purl across.

Work 4 rows in Stockinette Stitch.

Change to smallest size needles.

Instructions continued on page 16.

Turning Ridge: Purl across.

Work 4 rows in Stockinette Stitch.

Buttonhole Row: ★ Purl across to same place as buttonhole on Row 4, bind off next 2 sts; repeat from ★ 3{4-4-5} times **more**, purl across.

Buttonhole Row: ★ Knit across to bound off sts, **turn**; add on 2 sts, **turn**; repeat from ★ 3{4-4-5} times **more**, knit across.

Work 3 rows in Stockinette Stitch.

Bind off all sts in **knit**.

Using photo as a guide, thread yarn needle with Color A and weave needle through sts over slipped sts on Ridge Row.

Fold Buttonhole Band to **wrong** side along Turning Ridge and whipstitch in place.

With matching thread, sew around buttonholes, working through **both** thicknesses.

Sew shoulder seams.

COLLAR
With **right** side facing, medium size needles and Color B, pick up 4 sts across Buttonhole Band working through both thicknesses, pick up 11{15-17-17} sts along Right Front Neck Shaping, pick up 4 sts along Back Neck Shaping, pick up 18{18-18-22} sts across Back Neck, pick up 4 sts along Back Neck Shaping, pick up 11{15-17-17} sts along Left Front Neck Shaping, pick up 4 sts across Button Band working through both thicknesses: 56{64-68-72} sts.

Work in Garter Stitch for 1½{1¾-2-2}"/ 4{4.5-5-5} cm, increasing one st at each end of every fourth row.

Change to largest size needles.

Continue in Garter Stitch for 1½{1¾-2-2}"/ 4{4.5-5-5} cm, maintaining increases as before.

Bind off all sts **loosely** in **knit**.

FINISHING
Matching center of last row on Sleeve to shoulder seam, sew top of Sleeve along Armhole edge and sides of Sleeve to bound off edges (see Diagram).

Weave underarm and side in one continuous seam (Fig. 13, page 47).

Using photo as a guide, thread yarn needle with Color A and weave needle through sts over slipped sts on Ridge Rows.

Fold lower edge of Jacket to **wrong** side along Turning Ridge and whipstitch in place.

Using photo as a guide for placement, sew Pockets to Fronts.
Sew buttons to Button Band opposite buttonholes.

HAT
BAND
With largest size needles and Color B, cast on 68{68-75-75} sts.

DIAGRAM

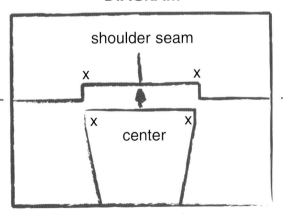

Work in Garter Stitch (knit every row) until Band measures 2{2-2½-2½}"/5{5-6.5-6.5} cm; cut yarn leaving a long end for sewing.

BODY
Change to medium size needles and MC.

Row 1: Knit across increasing 6{6-7-7} sts evenly spaced *(see Increasing Evenly and Figs. 2a & b, page 42)*: 74{74-82-82} sts.

Row 2: Purl across.

Row 3 - Ridge Row: K2, (slip 1 as if to **purl** with yarn in front, K1) across.

Continue in Stockinette Stitch until Hat measures approximately 5½{5½-6-6}"/14{14-15-15} cm from cast on edge, ending by working a **wrong** side row.

CROWN SHAPING
Row 1 (Decrease row): K1, K2 tog *(Fig. 7, page 44)*, (K6, K2 tog) across to last 7 sts, knit across: 65{65-72-72} sts.

Row 2: Purl across.

Row 3 (Decrease row): K1, K2 tog, (K5, K2 tog) across to last 6 sts, knit across: 56{56-62-62} sts.

Continue to decrease every other row, having one less st between each decrease, 4 times, ending by working a **wrong** side row: 20{20-22-22} sts.

Last Row: K1, K2 tog across to last st, K1; cut yarn leaving a long end for sewing: 11{11-12-12} sts.

FINISHING
Thread yarn needle with long end and weave through remaining sts on last row; gather tightly and secure.
Sew seam.

Using photo as a guide, thread yarn needle with Color A and weave needle through sts over slipped sts on Ridge Row.

Instructions continued on page 18.

MUFF
BODY

With medium size needles and MC, cast on 34{36-38-40} sts.

Work in Stockinette Stitch until piece measures approximately 8{9½-10-11}"/20.5{24-25.5-28} cm from cast on edge, ending by working a **wrong** side row; cut yarn leaving a long end for sewing.

Change to largest size needles and Color B.

Work in Garter Stitch (knit every row) until piece measures approximately 16{19-20-22}"/40.5{48.5-51-56} cm from cast on edge; cut yarn leaving a long end for sewing.

Bind off all sts in **knit**.

STRAP

With smallest size needles and MC, cast on 5{5-7-7} sts.

Row 1 (Right side): K1 tbl *(Fig. 1b, page 12)*, [P1 tbl *(Fig. 1a, page 42)*, K1 tbl] across.

Row 2: P1 tbl, (K1 tbl, P1 tbl) across.

Repeat Rows 1 and 2 until Strap measures approximately 22{27-30-32}"/56{68.5-76-81.5} cm from cast on edge.

Bind off all sts in pattern.

FINISHING

With **right** side facing and matching colors, weave long edges of Muff together to form a tube *(Fig. 13, page 47)*.

Fold MC portion of Muff down inside Color B portion, and sew in place around side edge of tube.

Sew 1" (2.5 cm) of each end of Strap to inside (MC portion) of tube, covering inner seam, and stitching securely all around end of Strap.

SCARF

BAND

With largest size needles and Color B, cast on 16{20-20-24} sts.

Work in Garter Stitch (knit every row) until Band measures 2{2-2$\frac{1}{2}$-2$\frac{1}{2}$}"/5{5-6.5-6.5} cm.

BODY

Change to medium size needles and MC.

Row 1: Knit across increasing 3 sts evenly spaced (*see Increasing Evenly and Figs. 2a & b, page 42*): 19{23-23-27} sts.

Row 2: Purl across.

Row 3 - Ridge Row: K1, (slip 1 as if to **purl** with yarn in front, K1) across.

Work in Stockinette Stitch until Scarf measures approximately 35$\frac{1}{2}${39$\frac{1}{2}$-42$\frac{1}{2}$-46$\frac{1}{2}$}"/90{100.5-108-118} cm from cast on edge, ending by working a **wrong** side row.

Ridge Row: K1, (slip 1 as if to **purl** with yarn in front, K1) across.

Next Row: Purl across.

Last Row: Knit across decreasing 3 sts evenly spaced (*Fig. 7, page 44*): 16{20-20-24} sts.

BAND

Change to largest size needles and Color B.

Row 1: Purl across.

Work in Garter Stitch until Band measures 2{2-2$\frac{1}{2}$-2$\frac{1}{2}$}"/5{5-6.5-6.5} cm.

Bind off all sts in **knit**.

Using photo as a guide, thread yarn needle with Color A and weave needle through sts over slipped sts on Ridge Rows.

OPTION 1

A medley of **turquoise** and purple on a background of rich cream creates a sweep of **softness** that she'll want to wear **everyday** — so it may be good idea to knit a second poncho set for weekends!

A **romp** of rich color, this fun outfit echoes the wearer's joyful nature. The matching hat, scarf, and mittens will keep her warm on the **playground** while her imagination takes flight.

OPTION ②

Plymouth "Encore"
Medium/Worsted Weight Yarn
[3½ ounces, 200 yards
(100 grams, 183 meters) per skein]
 MC: #218 Cream - 7 skeins
 Color A: #1033 Lavender - 2 skeins
 Color B: #235 Bright Turquoise - 2 skeins
 Color C: #1034 Dark Purple - 2 skeins
 Color D: #9401 Medium Teal - 2 skeins

Straight knitting needles, size 9 (5.5 mm) **or** size
 needed for gauge
16" (40.5 cm) Circular needle, size 7 (4.5 mm)
29" (73.5 cm) Circular needles, sizes 7 (4.5 mm)
 and 9 (5.5 mm) **or** sizes needed for gauge
Crochet hook, size H (5 mm) for fringe
Stitch holders - 2
Markers
Yarn needle

DE COLORES

 EASY

Caron® Simply Soft®
Medium/Worsted Weight Yarn
[6 ounces, 330 yards (170 grams, 302 yards)
per skein for solid colors **or** 4 ounces,
208 yards (114 grams, 190 meters) per skein for ombre]
 MC: #9811 Embroidery Prints - 5 skeins
 Color B: #9749 Jonquil - 1 skein
 Color C: #9748 Rubine Red - 1 skein
Caron® Simply Soft® Brites
Medium/Worsted Weight Yarn
[6 ounces, 330 yards (170 grams, 302 yards) per skein]
 Color A: #9608 Blue Mint - 1 skein
 Color D: #9610 Grape - 1 skein

Straight knitting needles, size 9 (5.5 mm) **or** size
 needed for gauge
16" (40.5 cm) Circular needle, size 7 (4.5 mm)
29" (73.5 cm) Circular needles, sizes 7 (4.5 mm)
 and 9 (5.5 mm) **or** sizes needed for gauge
Crochet hook, size H (5 mm) for fringe
Stitch holders - 2
Markers
Yarn needle

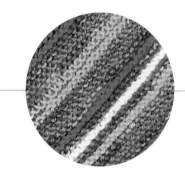

Sizes: 2{4-6-8}

Note: Instructions are written for size 2 with sizes 4, 6, 8 in braces { }. Instructions will be easier to read if you circle all the numbers pertaining to your child's size. If only one number is given, it applies to all sizes.

FINISHED MEASUREMENTS

PONCHO
Each Rectangle:
9{10-11-12}" wide x 18{20-22-24}" long
[23{25.5-28-30.5} cm x 45.5{51-56-61} cm]

HAT
Finished Circumference:
17{17-18³/₄-18³/₄}" / 43{43-47.5-47.5} cm

MITTENS
Finished Hand Circumference:
5¹/₂{6-6¹/₂-7}"/14{15-16.5-18} cm

SCARF
Finished Measurements:
4{5-5-6}" wide x 40{44-48-52}" long
10{12.5-12.5-15} cm x 101.5{112-122-132} cm

STRIPE SEQUENCE
2 Rows of each: ★ Color A, MC, Color B, MC, Color C, MC, Color D, MC; repeat from ★ throughout.

GAUGE
With larger size needles,
in Garter Stitch (knit every row),
17 sts and 35 rows = 4" (10 cm)

Instructions begin on page 24.

23

Row 2: Knit across.

Row 3 (Decrease row): With next color, SSK, ★ knit across to within 2 sts of marker, K2 tog, SSK; repeat from ★ 2 times **more**, knit across to last 2 sts, K2 tog: 228{252-276-300} sts.

Row 4: Knit across.

Rows 5-38{42-46-50}: Repeat Rows 3 and 4, 17{19-21-23} times: 92{100-108-116} sts.

Bind off remaining sts.

FINISHING
With **wrong** sides of bound off row together and next color, weave seam (*Fig. 13, page 47*). Sew corner seam.

Using diagram as a guide for placement, sew rectangles together.

FRINGE
Holding 3 strands of MC, each 12" (30.5 cm) long, and using photo as a guide for placement, add fringe around entire outer edge of Poncho (*Figs. 14a & b, page 47*).

PONCHO
RECTANGLE (Make 2)
With larger size 29" (73.5 cm) circular needle and Color A, cast on 244{268-292-316} sts.

Row 1 (Right side): SSK (*Figs. 8a-c, page 45*), K 38{42-46-50}, K2 tog (*Fig. 7, page 44*), place marker (*see Markers, page 40*), SSK, K 76{84-92-100}, K2 tog, place marker, SSK, K 38{42-46-50}, K2 tog, place marker, SSK, knit across to last 2 sts, K2 tog: 236{260-284-308} sts.

*Note: Loop a short piece of yarn around any stitch to mark Row 1 as **right** side.*

DIAGRAM

HAT
BAND

With smaller size 29" (73.5 cm) circular needle and Color A, cast on 172{172-188-188} sts.

Row 1 (Right side): SSK (*Figs. 8a-c, page 45*), K8, K2 tog (*Fig. 7, page 44*), place marker (*see Markers, page 40*), SSK, K 70{70-78-78}, K2 tog, place marker, SSK, K8, K2 tog, place marker, SSK, knit across to last 2 sts, K2 tog: 164{164-180-180} sts.

Note: Loop a short piece of yarn around any stitch to mark Row 1 as **right** side.

Row 2: Knit across.

Row 3 (Decrease row): With next color, SSK, ★ knit across to within 2 sts of marker, K2 tog, SSK; repeat from ★ 2 times **more**, knit across to last 2 sts, K2 tog: 156{156-172-172} sts.

Row 4: Knit across.

Rows 5-8: Repeat Rows 3 and 4 twice: 140{140-156-156} sts.

Bind off remaining sts.

With **wrong** sides of bound off row together and next color, weave seam (*Fig. 13, page 47*). Sew corner seam.

BODY

With **right** side facing, MC and straight needles, pick up 74{74-82-82} sts across one long edge of Band (*Fig. 11b, page 46*).

Work in Garter Stitch (knit every row) until Body measures approximately 4{4-4$\frac{1}{2}$-4$\frac{1}{2}$}"/ 10{10-11.5-11.5} cm, ending by working a **wrong** side row.

CROWN SHAPING

Row 1 (Decrease row): K1, K2 tog, (K6, K2 tog) 8{8-9-9} times, K7: 65{65-72-72} sts.

Row 2: Knit across.

Row 3 (Decrease row): K1, K2 tog, (K5, K2 tog) 8{8-9-9} times, K6: 56{56-62-62} sts.

Row 4: Knit across.

Continue to decrease every other row, having one less stitch between each decrease, 4 times, ending by working a **wrong** side row: 20{20-22-22} sts.

Last Row: K1, K2 tog across to last st, K1; cut yarn leaving a long end for sewing: 11{11-12-12} sts.

FINISHING

Thread yarn needle with long end and weave needle through remaining sts; gather tightly and secure. Sew seam.

Instructions continued on page 26.

MITTEN (Make 2)

CUFF

With 16" (40.5 cm) circular needle and Color A, cast on 68{72-76-80} sts.

Row 1 (Right side)**:** SSK *(Figs. 8a-c, page 45)*, K8, K2 tog *(Fig. 7, page 44)*, place marker *(see Markers, page 40)*, SSK, K 18{20-22-24}, K2 tog, place marker, SSK, K8, K2 tog, place marker, SSK, knit across to last 2 sts, K2 tog: 60{64-68-72} sts.

Note: Loop a short piece of yarn around any stitch to mark Row 1 as **right** side.

Row 2: Knit across.

Row 3: With next color, SSK, ★ knit across to within 2 sts of marker, K2 tog, SSK; repeat from ★ 2 times **more**, knit across to last 2 sts, K2 tog: 52{56-60-64} sts.

Row 4: Knit across.

Rows 5-8: Repeat Rows 3 and 4 twice: 36{40-44-48} sts.

Bind off remaining sts in **knit**.

With **wrong** sides of bound off row together and next color, weave seam *(Fig. 13, page 47)*. Sew corner seam.

HAND

With **right** side facing, MC and straight needles, pick up 23{25-27-29} sts across one long edge of Cuff *(Fig. 11b, page 46)*.

Knit 7{11-13-15} rows (Garter Stitch).

THUMB GUSSET

Row 1 (Right side)**:** K 11{12-13-14}, place marker, M1 *(Figs. 4a & b, page 43)*, K1, M1, place marker, K11{12-13-14}: 25{27-29-31} sts.

Knit 5{5-3-3} rows.

Increase Row: Knit across to marker, slip marker, M1, knit across to next marker, M1, slip marker, knit across: 27{29-31-33} sts.

Continue in Garter Stitch, increasing in same manner, every 6{6-4-4} rows, 2{2-3-3} times **more**: 31{33-37-39} sts.

Knit 1{3-5-5} row(s).

Cut yarn.

THUMB

Slip 11{12-13-14} sts onto st holder, with MC add on one st *(Figs. 5a & b, page 43)*, K9{9-11-11} sts, add on one st, slip remaining 11{12-13-14} sts onto second st holder: 11{11-13-13} sts.

Knit 3{5-9-9} rows.

SHAPING

Row 1: K1, K2 tog twice, K1{1-3-3}, K2 tog twice, K1: 7{7-9-9} sts.

Row 2: Knit across.

SIZES {6-8} ONLY

Row 3: K1, K2 tog, K3, K2 tog, K1: 7 sts.

Row 4: Knit across.

ALL SIZES

Row 3{3-5-5}: K1, (K2 tog, K1) twice; cut yarn leaving a long end for sewing: 5 sts.

Thread yarn needle with long end and weave needle through remaining 5 sts; gather tightly and secure.
Weave seam *(Fig. 13, page 47)*.

BODY

With **right** side facing, slip 11{12-13-14} sts from st holder onto straight needles, with MC knit across, pick up 2 sts at base of Thumb, slip 11{12-13-14} sts from second st holder onto empty needle and knit across: 24{26-28-30} sts.

Work even until piece measures approximately 5{6-7-8}"/12.5{15-18-20.5} cm from beginning of Cuff, ending by working a **wrong** side row.

SHAPING

Row 1: K1, SSK, K7{8-9-10} sts, K2 tog, place marker, SSK, K7{8-9-10} sts, K2 tog, K1: 20{22-24-26} sts.

Rows 2-4: Knit across.

Row 5: K1, SSK, knit across to within 2 sts of marker, K2 tog, SSK, knit across to last 3 sts, K2 tog, K1: 16{18-20-22} sts.

Row 6: Knit across.

Rows 7-10: Repeat Rows 5 and 6 twice: 8{10-12-14} sts.

SIZES {4-6-8} ONLY

Row 11: K1, SSK, K{0-1-2} *(see Zeros, page 40)*, K2 tog, SSK, K{0-1-2}, K2 tog, K1: {6-8-10} sts.

Row 12: Knit across.

SIZE 8 ONLY:

Row 13: K1, (SSK, K2 tog) twice, K1: 6 sts.

ALL SIZES

Cut yarn leaving a long end for sewing. Thread yarn needle with long end and weave needle through remaining sts; gather tightly and secure.
Weave seam.

SCARF

With larger size 29" (73.5 cm) circular needle and Color A, cast on 384{428-460-504} sts.

Row 1 (Right side): SSK *(Figs. 8a-c, page 45)*, K 18{22-22-26}, K2 tog *(Fig. 7, page 44)*, place marker *(see Markers, page 40)*, SSK, K 166{184-200-218}, K2 tog, place marker, SSK, K 18{22-22-26}, K2 tog, place marker, SSK, knit across to last 2 sts, K2 tog: 376{420-452-496} sts.

Row 2: Knit across.

Row 3 (Decrease row): With next color, SSK, ★ knit across to within 2 sts of marker, K2 tog, SSK; repeat from ★ 2 times **more**, knit across to last 2 sts, K2 tog: 368{412-444-488} sts.

Row 4: Knit across.

Rows 5 thru 18{22-22-26}: Repeat Rows 3 and 4, 7{9-9-11} times: 312{340-372-400} sts.

Bind off remaining sts.

With **wrong** sides of bound off row together and next color, weave seam *(Fig. 13, page 47)*.
Sew corner seam.

FINISHING
FRINGE

Holding 3 strands of MC, each 12" (30.5 cm) long, and using photo as a guide for placement, add fringe across short edges of Scarf *(Figs. 14a & b, page 47)*.

This vintage-style swing coat, scarf, hat, and mitten set is knit in modern **crayon** colors. Easy blanket stitches create cute little accents on **patches** and pockets. It's an updated fashion for your thoroughly modern girl.

OPTION 2

Knit in hues that are true to its **1930s** style, the patch-pocket swing coat and its matching accessories will inspire **compliments** everywhere she goes.

Option 1

Red Heart Kids
Medium/Worsted Weight Yarn
  [5 ounces, 302 yards
  (141 grams, 276 meters) per skein]
  MC: #2734 Pink - 3{4-4-5} skeins
  Color A: #2652 Lime - 2{2-3-3} skeins
  Color B: #2230 Yellow - 1 skein
Straight knitting needles, sizes 7 (4.5 mm) and 9
  (5.5 mm) **or** sizes needed for gauge
Stitch holders - 2
Markers
7/8" (22 mm) Buttons - 5{5-6-7}
Sewing needle and thread
Yarn needle

MEDIUM 4

NEVER A PATCH ON YOU 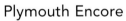 EASY

Option 2

Plymouth Encore
  Medium/Worsted Weight Yarn
  [3 1/2 ounces, 200 yards
  (100 grams, 183 meters) per skein]
    MC: #256 Off-White - 5{6-7-8} skeins
    Color A: #217 Black - 3{4-5-5} skeins
    Color B: #1203 Khaki - 1 skein
Straight knitting needles, sizes 7 (4.5 mm) 9
  (5.5 mm) **or** sizes needed for gauge
Stitch holders - 2
Markers
3/4" (19 mm) Buttons - 5{5-6-7}
Sewing needle and thread
Yarn needle

MEDIUM 4

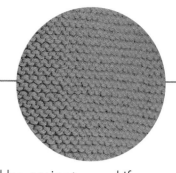

Sizes: 4{6-8-10}

Note: Instructions are written for size 4 with sizes 6, 8, 10 in braces { }. Instructions will be easier to read if you circle all the numbers pertaining to your child's size. If only one number is given, it applies to all sizes.

FINISHED MEASUREMENTS

COAT
Finished Chest Measurement: 29{31-33-35}"/
73.5{78.5-84-89} cm

MITTENS
Finished Hand Circumference:
5$^1/_2${6-6$^1/_2$-7}"/14{15-16.5-18} cm

SCARF
Finished Measurements:
4{5-5-6}" wide x 40{44-48-52}" long/
10{12.5-12.5-15} cm x 101.5{112-122-132} cm

HAT
Finished Circumference:
17{18$^3/_4$-18$^3/_4$-20$^3/_4$}"/43{47.5-47.5-52.5} cm

GAUGE
In Garter Stitch (knit every row),
with larger size needles,
17 sts and 35 rows = 4" (10 cm)

Instructions begin on page 32.

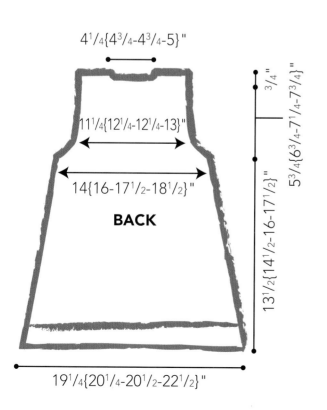

4$^1/_4${4$^3/_4$-4$^3/_4$-5}"

11$^1/_4${12$^1/_4$-12$^1/_4$-13}"

14{16-17$^1/_2$-18$^1/_2$}"

BACK

$^3/_4$"

5$^3/_4${6$^3/_4$-7$^1/_4$-7$^3/_4$}"

13$^1/_2${14$^1/_2$-16-17$^1/_2$}"

19$^1/_4${20$^1/_4$-20$^1/_2$-22$^1/_2$}"

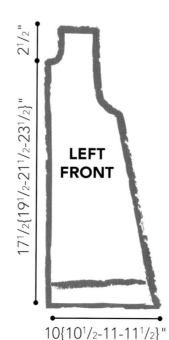

2$^1/_2$"

17$^1/_2${19$^1/_2$-21$^1/_2$-23$^1/_2$}"

LEFT FRONT

10{10$^1/_2$-11-11$^1/_2$}"

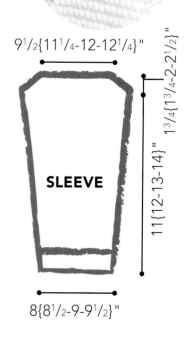

9$^1/_2${11$^1/_4$-12-12$^1/_4$}"

1$^3/_4${1$^3/_4$-2-2$^1/_2$}"

11{12-13-14}"

SLEEVE

8{8$^1/_2$-9-9$^1/_2$}"

COAT
BACK
BAND
With smaller size needles and Color A, cast on 82{86-92-96} sts.

Row 1 (Wrong side): Knit across.

Knit 7 rows (Garter Stitch).

BODY
Change to larger size needles and MC.

Work in Garter Stitch, decreasing one stitch at **each** edge (see Decreases, pages 45 and 46), every 10{12-14-14} rows, 9 times: 64{68-74-78} sts.

Work even until Back measures approximately 13$\frac{1}{2}${14$\frac{1}{2}$-16-17$\frac{1}{2}$}"/ 34.5{37-40.5-44.5} cm from cast on edge, ending by working a **wrong** side row.

Armhole Shaping
Row 1 (Decrease row): K1, SSK (Figs. 8a-c, page 45), knit across to last 3 sts, K2 tog (Fig. 7, page 44), K1: 62{66-72-76} sts.

Row 2: Knit across.

Rows 3 thru 16{16-22-22}: Repeat Rows 1 and 2, 7{7-10-10} times: 48{52-52-56} sts.

Work even until Back measures approximately 19$\frac{1}{4}${21$\frac{1}{4}$-23$\frac{1}{4}$-25$\frac{1}{4}$}"/ 49{54-59-64} cm from cast on edge, ending by working a **wrong** side row.

Neck Shaping
Both sides of Neck are worked at the same time, using separate yarn for **each** side.

Row 1: K 17{18-18-19} sts; with second yarn, K 14{16-16-18} sts, slip sts just worked onto st holder, knit across: 17{18-18-19} sts **each** side.

Row 2: Knit across.

Row 3 (Decrease row): Knit across to within 3 sts of Neck edge, K2 tog, K1; with second yarn, K1, SSK, knit across: 16{17-17-18} sts **each** side.

Rows 4 and 5: Repeat Rows 2 and 3: 15{16-16-17} sts on **each** side.

Work even until Back measures approximately 20{22-24-26}"/51{56-61-66} cm from cast on edge, ending by working a **wrong** side row.

Bind off all sts in **knit**.

LEFT FRONT
BAND
With smaller size needles and Color A, cast on 43{45-47-49} sts.

Row 1 (Wrong side): Knit across.

Knit 7 rows.

BODY
Change to larger size needles and MC.

Work in Garter Stitch, decreasing one stitch at side edge, every 10{12-14-14} rows, 9 times: 34{36-38-40} sts.

Work even until Left Front measures same as Back to Armhole Shaping, ending by working a **wrong** side row.

Armhole Shaping
Row 1 (Decrease row): K1, SSK, knit across: 33{35-37-39} sts.

Row 2: Knit across.

Rows 3 thru 16{16-22-22}: Repeat Rows 1 and 2, 7{7-10-10} times: 26{28-27-29} sts.

Work even until Left Front measures approximately 17$\frac{1}{2}${19$\frac{1}{2}$-21$\frac{1}{2}$-23$\frac{1}{2}$}"/ 44.5{49.5-54.5-59.5} cm from cast on edge, ending by working a **right** side row.

Neck Shaping
Row 1: Bind off 7{8-7-8} sts, knit across: 19{20-20-21} sts.

Row 2: Knit across.

Row 3 (Decrease row): K1, K2 tog, knit across: 18{19-19-20} sts.

Rows 4 and 5: Repeat Rows 1 and 2: 17{18-18-19} sts.

Rows 6-8: Knit across.

Row 9 (Decrease row): K1, K2 tog, knit across: 16{17-17-18} sts.

Rows 10-13: Repeat Rows 6-9: 15{16-16-17} sts.

Work even until Left Front measures same as Back, ending by working a **wrong** side row.

Bind off all sts in **knit**.

Instructions continued on page 34.

Instructions continued on page 34.

RIGHT FRONT

BAND

With smaller size needles and Color A, cast on 43{45-47-49} sts.

Row 1 (Wrong side): Knit across.

Knit 7 rows.

BODY

Change to larger size needles and MC.

Working in Garter Stitch, decrease one stitch at **side** edge, every 10{12-14-14} row, 9 times: 34{36-38-40} sts.

Work even until Right Front measures same as Back to Armhole Shaping, ending by working a **right** side row.

Armhole Shaping

Row 1 (Decrease row): K1, K2 tog, knit across: 33{35-37-39} sts.

Row 2: Knit across.

Rows 3 thru 16{16-18-22}: Repeat Rows 1 and 2, 7{7-8-10} times: 26{28-29-29} sts.

Work even until Right Front measures same as Left Front to Neck Shaping, ending by working a **wrong** side row.

Neck Shaping

Row 1: Bind off 7{8-7-8} sts, knit across. 19{20-20-21} sts.

Row 2: Knit across.

Row 3 (Decrease row): K1, SSK, knit across: 18{19-19-20} sts.

Rows 4 and 5: Repeat Rows 2 and 3: 17{18-18-19} sts.

Rows 6-8: Knit across.

Row 9 (Decrease row): K1, SSK, knit across: 16{17-17-18} sts.

Rows 10-13: Repeat Rows 6-9: 15{16-16-17} sts.

Work even until Right Front measures same as Back, ending by working a **wrong** side row.

Bind off all sts in **knit**.

SLEEVE (Make 2)

BAND

With smaller size needles and Color B, cast on 34{36-38-40} sts.

Row 1 (Wrong side): Knit across.

Knit 7 rows.

BODY

Change to larger size needles and Color A.

Work in Garter Stitch, increasing one stitch at **each** edge (*Figs. 2a & b, page 42*), every fourth row, 0{6-4-6} times (*see Zeros, page 40*); then increase every sixth row, 11{8-11-11} times: 56{64-68-74} sts.

Work even until Sleeve measures approximately 11{12-13-14}"/ 28{30.5-33-35.5} cm from cast on edge, ending by working a **wrong** side row.

SLEEVE CAP

Row 1: K1, SSK, knit across to last 3 sts, K2 tog, K1: 54{62-66-72} sts.

Row 2: Knit across.

Rows 3 thru 16{16-18-22}: Repeat Rows 1 and 2, 7{7-8-10} times: 40{48-50-52} sts.

Bind off remaining sts in **knit**.

POCKET (Make 2)

With larger size needles and Color B, cast on 11 sts.

Working in Garter Stitch, increase one stitch at each edge, every other row, 3{3-6-6} times: 17{17-23-23} sts.

Work even until Pocket measures 4{5-5-5¹/₂}"/ 10{12.5-12.5-14} cm from cast on edge, ending by working a **wrong** side row.

Bind off all sts in **knit**.

FINISHING

Sew shoulder seams.

NECKBAND

With **right** side facing, smaller size needles, and Color A, pick up 18{18-19-19} sts along Right Front Neck Shaping *(Figs. 11a & b, page 46)*, pick up 4 sts along Back Neck Shaping, pick up 14{16-16-18} sts across Back Neck, pick up 4 sts along Back Neck Shaping, pick up 18{18-19-19} sts along Front Neck Shaping: 58{60-62-64} sts.

Work in Garter Stitch for 8 rows.

Bind off all sts in **knit**.

BUTTON BAND

With **right** side facing, smaller size needles, and Color A, beginning at top edge of Neckband, pick up 79{87-95-105} sts evenly spaced along Left Front edge.

Knit 7 rows.

Bind off all sts in **knit**.

BUTTONHOLE BAND

With **right** side facing, smaller size needles, and Color A, pick up {79-87}{95-105-113} sts evenly spaced along Right Front edge to top of Neckband.

Rows 1-3: Knit across.

Mark placement of buttonholes, placing markers ¹/₂" (12 mm) from neck edge and 1³/₄" (4.5 cm) from bottom edge. Evenly space 3{3-4-5} markers for remaining buttons.

Row 4 (Buttonhole row): ★ Knit across to next marker, remove marker, bind off next 2 sts; repeat from ★ 4{4-5-6} times **more**, knit across.

Row 5 (Buttonhole row): ★ Knit across to bound off sts, **turn**; add on 2 sts *(Figs. 5a & b, page 43)*, **turn**; repeat from ★ 4{4-5-6} times **more**, knit across.

Rows 6 and 7: Knit across.

Bind off all sts in **knit**.

Set in Sleeves matching center of Sleeve to shoulder seam.

Weave side and underarm in one continuous seam *(Fig. 13, page 47)*.

Instructions continued on page 36.

HAND
With MC, knit 12{14-16-16} rows.

THUMB GUSSET
Change to larger size needles.

Row 1 (Right side): K 12{13-14-15}, place marker (*see Markers, page 40*), M1 (*Figs. 4a & b, page 43*), K1, M1, place marker, K 12{13-14-15}: 27{29-31-33} sts.

Knit 5{3-3-3} rows.

Increase Row: Knit across to marker, slip marker, M1, knit across to next marker, M1, slip marker, knit across: 29{31-33-35} sts.

Work in Garter Stitch, increasing in same manner, every 6{4-4-4} rows, 2{3-3-3} times **more**: 33{37-39-41} sts.

Knit 1{3-5-5} row(s).

Cut yarn.

THUMB
Slip 12{13-14-15} sts onto st holder, with MC add on one st (*Figs. 5a & b, page 43*), K9{9-11-11} sts, add on one st, slip remaining 12{13-14-15} sts onto second st holder: 12{13-14-15} sts.

Knit 5{5-9-9} rows.

SHAPING
Row 1: K1, K2 tog twice (*Fig. 7, page 44*), K1{1-3-3}, K2 tog twice, K1: 7{7-9-9} sts.

Row 2: Knit across.

SIZES {8-10} ONLY
Row 3: K1, K2 tog, K3, K2 tog, K1: 7 sts.

Row 4: Knit across.

ALL SIZES
Row 3{3-5-5}: K1, (K2 tog, K1) twice: 5 sts.

Cut yarn leaving a long end for sewing. Thread yarn needle with long end and weave needle through remaining 5 sts; gather tightly and secure Weave seam (*Fig. 13, page 47*).

Using photo as a guide for placement:
Sew Pockets to Fronts, placing them 3{3-3-3$\frac{1}{2}$}"/ 7.5{7.5-7.5-9} cm in from front opening and at desired height from lower edge.

Thread yarn needle with Color A, work blanket stitch around entire edge of both Pockets (*Figs. 15a & b, page 47*). Sew buttons to Button Band opposite buttonholes.

MITTEN (Make 2)
BAND
With smaller size needles and Color A, cast on 25{27-29-29} sts.

Row 1 (Wrong side): Knit across.

Knit 7 rows (Garter Stitch).

BODY

With **right** side facing, slip 12{13-14-15} sts from st holder onto larger size needles, with MC knit across, pick up and knit 2 sts at base of Thumb *(Fig. 11b, page 46)*, slip 12{13-14-15} sts from second st holder onto empty needle and knit across: 26{28-30-32} sts.

Work even until piece measures approximately 6{7-8-8}"/14.5{16.5-18.5-18.5} cm from cast on edge, ending by working a **wrong** side row.

SHAPING

Row 1: K1, SSK *(Figs. 8a-c, page 45)*, K8{9-10-11} sts, K2 tog, place marker, SSK, K8{9-10-11} sts, K2 tog, K1: 22{24-26-28} sts.

Rows 2-4: Knit across.

Row 5: K1, SSK, knit across to within 2 sts of marker, K2 tog, SSK, knit across to last 3 sts, K2 tog, K1: 18{20-22-24} sts.

Row 6: Knit across.

Rows 7-10: Repeat Rows 5 and 6 twice: 10{12-14-16} sts.

Row 11: K1, SSK, K 0{1-2-3} sts *(see Zeros, page 40)*, K2 tog, SSK, K 0{1-2-3} sts, K2 tog, K1: 6{8-10-12} sts.

Row 12: Knit across.

SIZES {8-10} ONLY
Row 13: K1, SSK, K2 tog, K{0-2}, SSK, K2 tog, K1: {6-8} sts.

Row 14: Knit across.

ALL SIZES
Cut yarn leaving a long end for sewing. Thread yarn needle with long end and weave needle through remaining sts; gather tightly and secure. Weave seam.

POCKET (Make 2)

With larger size needles and Color B, cast on 8{9-10-10} sts.

Knit 3 rows.

Increase Row: Increase *(Figs. 2a & b, page 42)*, knit across to last st, increase: 10{11-12-12} sts.

Work even until Pocket measures 2$\frac{1}{2}${3-3$\frac{1}{2}$-3$\frac{1}{2}$}"/ 6.5{7.5-9-9} cm from cast on edge.

Bind off all sts in **knit**.

Instructions continued on page 38.

FINISHING
Using photo as a guide for placement:
Sew one Pocket to each Mitten on back side of hand.

With Color A, work blanket stitch (*Figs. 15a & b, page 47)* around each pocket.

SCARF
FIRST BAND
With larger size needles and Color B, cast on 17{21-21-26} sts.

Row 1 (Wrong side): Knit across.

Knit 18 rows (Garter Stitch).

BODY
Change to MC.

Work in Garter Stitch until Scarf measures approximately 38{42-46-50}"/96.5{106.5-117-127} cm from cast on edge, ending by working a **wrong** side row.

SECOND BAND
Change to Color B.

Knit 18 rows.

Bind off all sts in **knit**.

POCKET (Make 2)
With larger size needles and Color B, cast on 13{13-15-15} sts.

Work in Garter Stitch, increasing one stitch at **each** edge, every fourth row twice: 17{17-19-19} sts.

Work even until Pocket measures 4{5-5-5½}"/ 10{12.5-12.5-14} cm from cast on edge.

Bind off all sts in **knit**.

FINISHING
Using photo as a guide for placement:
Sew one Pocket to each end of Scarf with cast on edge of each Pocket 4" (10 cm) up from Scarf end.

Thread yarn needle with Color A and work blanket stitch around each Pocket and across Bands *(Figs. 15a & b, page 47).*

HAT
BAND
With smaller size needles and Color B, cast on 74{74-82-90} sts.

Rows 1-18: Knit across.

Cut yarn.

Row 19 (Right side)**:** With Color A, knit across.

BODY
Change to larger size needles and MC.

Work in Garter Stitch until Hat measures approximately 6{6½-7}"/15{16.5-18} cm from cast on edge, ending by working a **wrong** side row.

CROWN SHAPING
Row 1: K1, K2 tog *(Fig. 7, page 44)*, (K6, K2 tog) across to last 7 sts, K7: 65{65-72-79} sts.

Row 2: Knit across.

Row 3: K1, K2 tog, (K5, K2 tog) across to last 6 sts, K6: 56{56-62-68} sts.

Row 4: Knit across.

Row 5: K1, K2 tog, (K4, K2 tog) across to last 5 sts, K5: 47{47-52-57} sts.

Row 6: Knit across.

Row 7: K1, K2 tog, (K3, K2 tog) across to last 4 sts, K4: 38{38-42-46} sts.

Row 8: Knit across.

Row 9: (K2, K2 tog) across to last 3 sts, K3: 29{29-32-35} sts.

Row 10: Knit across.

Row 11: (K1, K2 tog) across to last 2 sts, K2: 20{20-22-24} sts.

Row 12: Knit across.

Row 13: K1, K2 tog across to last st, K1; cut yarn leaving long end for sewing: 11{11-12-13} sts

FINISHING
Thread needle with long end and weave yarn needle through remaining sts on last row; gather tightly and secure.
Weave seam *(Fig. 13, page 47).*

Using photo as a guide for placement, thread yarn needle with Color A, work blanket stitch around entire cast on edge of Band *(Figs. 15a & b, page 47).* Fold Band up.

GENERAL

ABBREVIATIONS

cm	centimeters	SSP	slip, slip, purl
K	knit	st(s)	stitch(es)
M1	make one	tbl	through back loop
mm	millimeters	tog	together
P	purl	YO	yarn over
SSK	slip, slip, knit		

( ) or [ ] — work enclosed instructions **as many**
   times as specified by the number immediately
   following **or** contains explanatory remarks.

colon (:) — the number(s) given after a colon at the
   end of a row or round denote(s) the number of stitches
   or spaces you should have on that row or round.

GAUGE

Exact gauge is **essential** for proper size. Before beginning
your project, make a sample swatch in the yarn and needle
specified. After completing the swatch, measure it, counting
your stitches and rows carefully. If your swatch is larger or
smaller than specified, **make another, changing needle size
to get the correct gauge.** Keep trying until you find the size
needles that will give you the specified gauge.

MARKERS

As a convenience to you, we have used markers to help
distinguish the beginning of a pattern. Place markers as
instructed. You may use purchased markers or tie a length of
contrasting color yarn around the needle. When you reach a
marker on each row, slip it from the left needle to the right
needle; remove it when no longer needed.

ZEROS

To consolidate the length of an involved pattern, Zeros are
sometimes used so that all sizes can be combined. For example,
increase one stitch at each edge, every 6th row, 0{3-7} times
means the first size would do nothing, the second size would
increase 3 times, and the largest size would increase 7 times.

INSTRUCTIONS

KNITTING NEEDLES

UNITED STATES	ENGLISH U.K.	METRIC (mm)
0	13	2
1	12	2.25
2	11	2.75
3	10	3.25
4	9	3.5
5	8	3.75
6	7	4
7	6	4.5
8	5	5
9	4	5.5
10	3	6
10½	2	6.5
11	1	8
13	00	9
15	000	10
17	---	12.75
19	---	15

KNIT TERMINOLOGY

UNITED STATES		INTERNATIONAL
gauge	=	tension
bind off	=	cast off
yarn over (YO)	=	yarn forward (yfwd) **or** yarn around needle (yrn)

Yarn Weight Symbol & Names	SUPER FINE 1	FINE 2	LIGHT 3	MEDIUM 4	BULKY 5	SUPER BULKY 6
Type of Yarns in Category	Sock, Fingering Baby	Sport, Baby	DK, Light Worsted	Worsted, Afghan, Aran	Chunky, Craft, Rug	Bulky, Roving
Knit Gauge Ranges in Stockinette St to 4" (10 cm)	27-32 sts	23-26 sts	21-24 sts	16-20 sts	12-15 sts	6-11 sts
Advised Needle Size Range	1-3	3-5	5-7	7-9	9-11	11 and larger

■□□□ BEGINNER		Projects for first-time knitters using basic knit and purl stitches. Minimal shaping.
■■□□ EASY		Projects using basic stitches, repetitive stitch patterns, simple color changes, and simple shaping and finishing.
■■■□ INTERMEDIATE		Projects with a variety of stitches, such as basic cables and lace, simple intarsia, double-pointed needles and knitting in the round needle techniques, mid-level shaping and finishing.
■■■■ EXPERIENCED		Projects using advanced techniques and stitches, such as short rows, fair isle, more intricate intarsia, cables, lace patterns, and numerous color changes.

THROUGH BACK LOOP
(abbreviated tbl)

Insert the **right** needle through the back loop of the next stitch *(Fig. 1a or Fig. 1b)*.

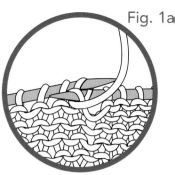

Fig. 1a

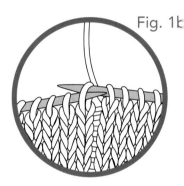

Fig. 1b

INCREASES
INCREASING EVENLY

Add one to the number of increases required and divide that number into the number of stitches on the needle. Subtract one from the result and the new number is the approximate number of stitches to be worked between each increase. Adjust the number as needed.

KNIT INCREASE

Knit the next stitch but do **not** slip the old stitch off the left needle *(Fig. 2a)*. Insert the right needle into the **back** loop of the **same** stitch and knit it *(Fig. 2b)*, then slip the old stitch off the left needle.

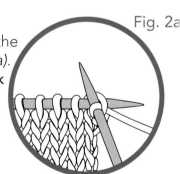

Fig. 2a

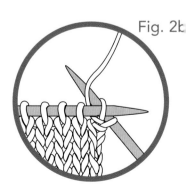

Fig. 2b

PURL INCREASE

Purl the next stitch but do **not** slip the old stitch off the left needle. Insert the right needle into the **back** loop of the **same** stitch from **back** to **front** (*Fig. 3*) and purl it. Slip the old stitch off the left needle.

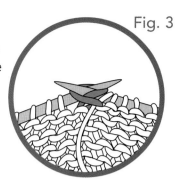

Fig. 3

MAKE ONE
(abbreviated M1)

Insert the **left** needle under the horizontal strand between the stitches from the front (Fig. 4a). Then knit into the **back** of the strand (Fig. 4b).

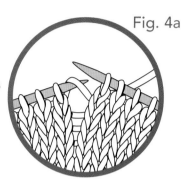

Fig. 4a

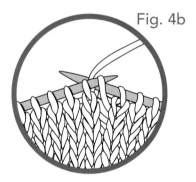

Fig. 4b

ADDING NEW STITCHES

Insert the right needle into stitch as if to **knit**, yarn over and pull loop through (*Fig. 5a*), insert the left needle into the loop just worked from **front** to **back** and slip the loop onto the left needle (*Fig. 5b*). Repeat for required number of stitches.

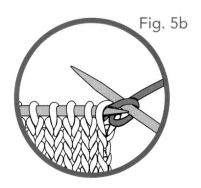

Fig. 5a

Fig. 5b

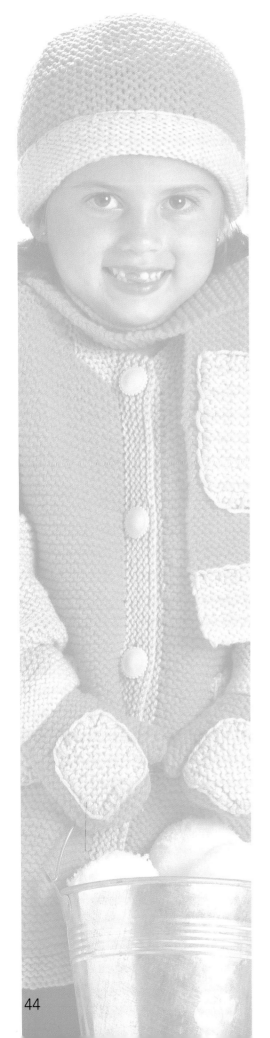

YARN OVERS
(abbreviated YO)
After a knit stitch, before a knit stitch
Bring the yarn forward **between** the
needles, then back **over** the top of
the right hand needle, so that it is
now in position to knit the next stitch
(Fig. 6a).

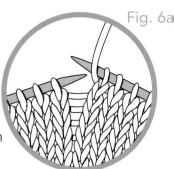

Fig. 6a

After a purl stitch, before a purl stitch
Take yarn **over** the right hand needle
to the back, then forward **under** it,
so that it is now in position to purl
the next stitch *(Fig. 6b)*.

Fig. 6b

KNIT 2 TOGETHER
(abbreviated K2 tog)
Insert the right needle into the **front**
of the first two stitches on the left
needle as if to **knit** *(Fig. 7)*, then
knit them together as if they were
one stitch.

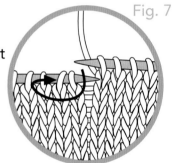

Fig. 7

SLIP, SLIP, KNIT
(abbreviated SSK)

With yarn in back of work, separately slip two stitches as if to **knit** *(Fig. 8a)*. Insert the **left** needle into the **front** of both slipped stitches *(Fig. 8b)* and knit them together as if they were one stitch *(Fig. 8c)*.

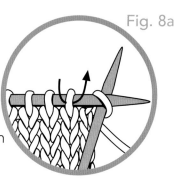

Fig. 8a

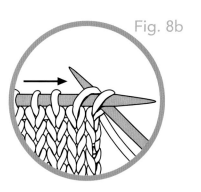

Fig. 8b

Fig. 8c

PURL 2 TOGETHER
(abbreviated P2 tog)

Insert the right needle into the **front** of the first two stitches on the left needle as if to **purl** *(Fig. 9)*, then **purl** them together as if they were one stitch.

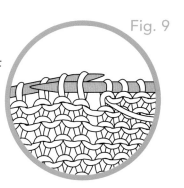

Fig. 9

SLIP, SLIP, PURL
(abbreviated SSP)

Separately slip two stitches as if to **knit**. Place these two stitches back onto the left needle. Insert the right needle into the **back** of both stitches from **back** to **front** *(Fig. 10)* and purl them together as they were one stitch.

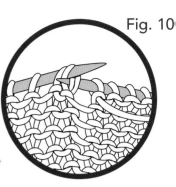

Fig. 10

PICKING UP STITCHES

When instructed to pick up stitches, insert the needle from the **front** to the **back** under two strands at the edge of the worked piece *(Figs. 11a & b)*. Put the yarn around the needle as if to **knit**, then bring the needle with the yarn back through the stitch to the right side, resulting in a stitch on the needle.
Repeat this along the edge, picking up the required number of stitches.
A crochet hook may be helpful to pull yarn through.

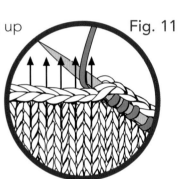

Fig. 11

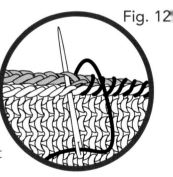

Fig. 11

WHIPSTITCH

With **right** sides together, sew through both pieces once to secure the beginning of the seam, leaving an ample yarn end to weave in later. Insert the needle from front to back through one strand on each piece *(Fig. 12)*. Bring the needle around and insert it from front to back through the next strand on both pieces.
Repeat along the edge, being careful to match rows or stitches.

Fig. 12

WEAVING SEAMS

With the **right** side of both pieces facing you and edges even, sew through both sides once to secure the seam. Insert the needle under the bar **between** the first and second stitches on the row and pull the yarn through (Fig. 13). Insert the needle under the next bar on the second side. Repeat from side to side, being careful to match rows.

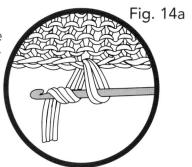

Fig. 13

FRINGE

Cut a piece of cardboard 3" (7.5 cm) wide and 6¹/₂" (16.5 cm). Wind the yarn **loosely** and **evenly** lengthwise around the cardboard until the card is filled, then cut across one end; repeat as needed. Hold together as many strands as specified in individual instructions; fold in half.

With **wrong** side facing and using a crochet hook, draw the folded end up through a stitch and pull the loose ends through the folded end (Fig. 14a); draw the knot up **tightly** (Fig. 14b). Repeat, spacing as specified in individual instructions.
Lay flat on a hard surface and trim the ends.

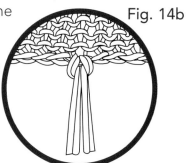

Fig. 14a

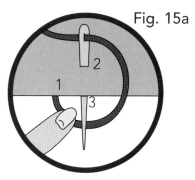

Fig. 14b

BLANKET STITCH

Bring the needle up at 1 (Fig. 15a). Keeping the yarn below the point of the needle, go down at 2 and come up at 3. Continue working (Fig. 15b).

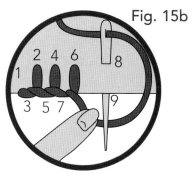

Fig. 15a

Fig. 15b

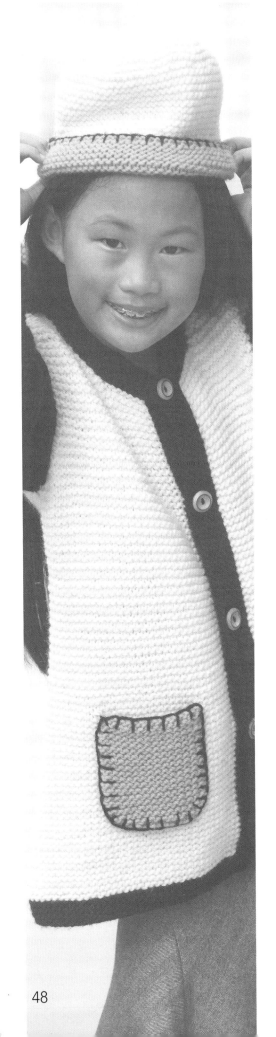

HINTS AND TIPS
GARTER STITCH
Garter Stitch is the result of knitting every stitch in every row. Two rows of knitting make one horizontal ridge in your fabric (Photo A).

Photo A

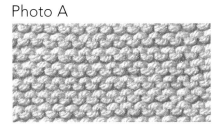

STOCKINETTE STITCH
Stockinette Stitch is the result of alternating knit and purl rows. The right side is smooth (Photo B) and the wrong side is bumpy (Photo C).

Photo B

Photo C

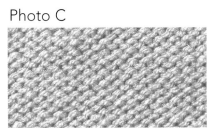

YARN ENDS
As in all garments, good finishing techniques make a big difference in the quality of the piece. Do not tie knots. Always start a new ball at the beginning of a row, leaving ends long enough to weave in later.

Thread a yarn needle with the yarn end. With wrong side facing, weave the needle through several inches, then reverse the direction and weave it back through several inches. When ends are secure, clip them off close to work.

BINDING OFF
Count stitches as you bind off: It takes two stitches to bind off one stitch. Count each stitch as you bind it off, not as you knit it.

Binding off in pattern: Unless otherwise stated, when you are instructed to bind off your stitches, you should always bind off in pattern. In reality, you are working another row.

Binding off loosely versus tightly: Bind off loosely for an edge with elasticity and bind off tightly for a firm edge.

Items made and instructions tested by Shawn Glidden, Judy Seip, Edwina Steel, Donna Warnell, and Jo Ellyn Wheeler.